NAZAR BOY

NAZAR BOY

Tarik Dobbs

Haymarket Books
Chicago, IL

Published in 2024 by
Haymarket Books
P.O. Box 180165
Chicago, IL 60618
773-583-7884
www.haymarketbooks.org
info@haymarketbooks.org

ISBN: 979-8-88890-089-5

Distributed to the trade in the US through Consortium Book Sales and Distribution
(www.cbsd.com) and internationally through Ingram Publisher Services International
(www.ingramcontent.com).

This book was published with the generous support of Lannan Foundation, Wallace Action
Fund, and the Marguerite Casey Foundation.

Special discounts are available for bulk purchases by organizations and institutions. Please
email info@haymarketbooks.org for more information.

Cover design by Matt Avery.

Library of Congress Cataloging-in-Publication data is available.

Printed in Canada

For my mother, our mothers

For Ahmad Hussein Shamseddine (1941–1971)

CONTENTS

LIVED HERE

My Birth State can't possibly drive interest

-ed parties, I insisted, on walking most days

Across the freeway medianed grocery store.

I wrote toward whatever fed my timed

Stays at universities. With this padded resumé, I resumed

Polite laughter in the next Zoomed room.

I watched some professors write from East

Villaged, a Vermont Somewhere'd

West of Hollywood, in a Martha'd

Vineyard. This year I read applications to be fellowshipped

—This particular, endowed lifestyle

Forbade applicants outside of the officially boroughed

New York Cities. My aunt asked how I lived,

I mentioned $300, gigged. For years I've ripped

All labeled information from my tagged seams,

Inched holes through every collar I hampered.

Years ago, I shared an attic'd bedroom. My piled clothing

On the floor next to my younger brother's bed. Unlaundered.

I was so depressed once I googled: maybe this Lake isn't

Oceaned. I told a novelist this and they flew to a Flyover State,

Then wrote sadness imaged. On a flight into Romulus, Michigan,

A man called a city, deteriorated. A professor lectured in Dearborn and

Called it Detroit. My mother lifted your luggage

At the appropriate countered space. A patron noticed

My mother wears her repetitive motioned injury.

Two doctors said it would be reparative if she quit her gigged

Life. Became a companioned, a

Compassioned transfer if she airported

To another airport. The benefited, most days,

I fly for less than a hundred dollars on a policy

Where I wear a pressed shirt and talk about the weathered,

Pardon. And I pardoned my way to the first-class lavatory

—The first classed lavatories always have hand lotion—

Or the main cabin is never lotioned. On the mini'd

Television, scientists are saying flying causes, for most, delayed

Bowel movements. There was always a man who coughed in the front row.

A slowed, white deathed. This man always thanked

In grand cabined speeches of diamond and medallioned. For safety,

My mother called me from the parking lot of a Home Depoted

Where a man called my mother beddable; men bother her at every aged

Year. If my mother isn't beautiful, men still decided it.

Once, I walked through the Beiruted terminal and tried to bribe an officer.

At 3 a.m., I walked through luggage unclaimed and found a pile of boxed cats,

Their gridded homes meowed forever into our quiet machined bunker.

Forever would've been forever'd if Another Country hadn't bombed the shit

Out of this Country's people's airport in 2006. Around 4 a.m. another plane

Landed. *Sssssssssssssssss*, My Sitto shushed the cats. Her gesture

Still Arabiced after being half-centuried

In America. One morning I told Sitto,

Before Colonizers said *The Ukraine*, they The'd Libnan.

A disambiguation—Nationed.

My mother said when she grew up the people of America forgot her placed.

She slept in an attic bedroomed and always jobbed. In memory,

My mother still her old passported. In the old Country,

The passport officed into a coffee shop, really, write this down:

There's poor recorded keeping with lots of emptied shelling.

I am the best cased scenario among many Countrymen. Men,

I learned them. Knew them.

Much of my decision-making is ruled,

Is laid across a tabled thought.

I am a poor scholared,

A brain correctly informationed. I used

To smoke Spice out of plastic bottles and printed paper;

I remember my sixth-grade apple bonged—

It was all so organics, so earthed. The winded said

Something to me like, weak lunged. I swallowed the roach

And clung toothed to a faucet head.

The fired fire it's evocative,

Each cigarello'd breath, breathed away. My

Mother at the café smiled into a webcam neither modern nor vintaged.

My mother sparkles like a mothered.

During one physical, a doctor held down my feet while I struggled

Into a sit-up. Once he said, faster. He come on'd

Me, as he gripped me. It endlessed.

My mother stands smiled into the morning afternoon evening'd.

Once I was so happy I ringed my own finger–

Stoned so bright, I couldn't see the flesh behind.

I worry about these deadened people. Us dogged

People. In the American terminal'd, it sounds like a dog is laughing.

The dogs victoried. Yes,

It snows in the old Country.

And I know

What I wasn't supposed to do here.

The eye of the gun is multi-pupiled. Blah blah went the angels, though they watched over us, didn't they? Or did we come to our aid?
    —ZEINA HASHEM BECK

POEM WHERE EVERY BIRD IS A DRONE

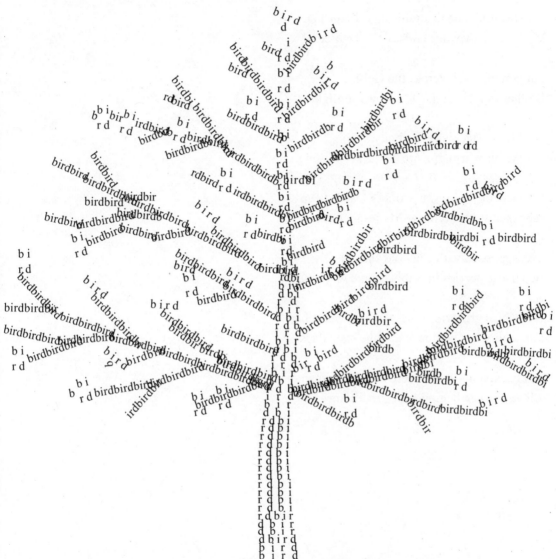

man has always envied the bird & now I envy the murder & now I murder the murder & now birds playback live on the air & now dead birds live in the air & now men call a murder *champagne* & now men call sign murder *champagne* & a man's fist pours a glass of *champagne* & now his bottle hisses & was it carbonation or the flutter of wings? & now they bird a house & now soldiers behind a desktop sing *champagne* & now they bird another house & now *champagne* & now they bird until a blackout & now the tree's murder is its own blackout & now a wall of murder & now the conspiracy comes true: a tree in which every bird is a drone.

MY BROTHER WAS BORN BOTH ALLY & COMBATANT

All voyeurism begins with surveillance ⊙
My brother's voyage ends in the Galilee

I dream of a wall across the Galilee ⊙
Brother tunnels under & follows sunlight

a hot light eats his entire body
⊙ Like his warm gun ate his jacket's lining

His jacket's lining was wool ⊙ Dead sheep
supposedly still living ⊙ My brother does

live, supposedly, like his old state ⊙
He buys groceries in Nablus some weekends

⊙ He buys groceries *for* Nablus on weekends ⊙
I hope this city begins where the state ends

that occupation ends where the state began ⊙
All voyeurism begins with surveillance

THE WIRE

In middle school there was a race war:
the white boys tried to drown Jamal in the pool.
Again, I am called by administrators to mediate
with my two planted wires, to diffuse,

to eat the bomb, a tie swings to me and says,
Tur-reek, you are a demolition expert,
bomb-proof container, and the boys
don't try drowning Jamal again. Instead,

the white boys get a pizza party.
Instead, they call me *faggot* and *terrorist.*
A self-destructing mechanism counts down
inside me; I pull the wires from my chest,

try to choose which to sever.

LISTENING TO THE NEWS ON YOUTUBE WITH COUNTRIES MISSING

ABC News broadcast from September 12, 2001, New York City, US

They can't push us around. Anything short of a violent response would be useless. The enemy has got to be eradicated. There was no stomach for restraint. I think these people are a bunch of

cowards and I worshipper at [redacted] *. and be done we can mosques in this phone calls. boiled over ... associated with hit? Would the it just make the war with us. The The* [redacted] *happens will not extremism there the aid workers out; they paid documents. There's anxiety is not why a few* [redacted] *, crimes. In fact, the Arabs see the of* [redacted] *repression of land and ... provocative control over stationing of Izlam's holiest against* [redacted] *, children of -thing has been* [redacted] *'s recent militants using gunships — response today. That is the price*

would love to ... A a downtown mosque Can we take out one with it? I don't think eradicate an entire area have received When people's Terrorism is not Izlam. Who or what [redacted] *inflict real feel better? loses the moral* [redacted] *suggested happen soon. There that worries the of the United Nations off their local staff We're going to stay in the region as a Muzlums would or why others would* [redacted] *is a target as an What they believe is* [redacted] *independence ... issues [are]: Izlamic holy sites in* [redacted] *troops ... sites; and economic which have seemed medicine and food. more infuriating to attacks on* [redacted] *- built prompting this kind Of course, I'm sorry for everything they*

[redacted] *supported or two people so. I don't think culture. Several threatening passions have automatically would the* [redacted] *pain? Or would Someone is at high ground. whatever is a strain of* [redacted] *. In have cleared and took their overseas. whole... But that murder so many applaud their because many accomplice the ruthless aspirations for The most* [redacted] *'s Jerusalem; the near some of sanctions to deprive But perhaps no many Arabs as* [redacted] *helicopters as of Arab for the civilians. did: the streets.*

I mean the streets have to pay the price for the suffering of the whole world. That rationale may seem irrational, but it is an explanation for yesterday's aftermath and is shared by many Arabs in the Middle East and elsewhere. It explains nothing and everything. Signing off, ABC News.

SYNDROME NAMESAKE WITH NO HISTORY FOUND

In 1840, Dr. Alfred Poland unearthed a dead man:
George Elt, prisoner of England, with no record
-ed history. Though guards noted: Elt couldn't reach

across his chest—no allegiances—
his history, now, a several page report: a body
generally sparse and delicate; his six ribs

inferior. On my left thigh, doctors left
an eternal ornament—tracing my scar, sometimes
it itches until it burns. Like torn-up duck feet,

my finger grafts are always catching and tearing
their hairs on phone edges, zippers, kettle lids.
In Poland's illustration, Elt's jaw is slightly

slack. A map for future subjects—my mother read
I had *an 8% chance of club foot* which mis-predicted
my clubbed thumb—flawed eugenics. Years ago,

George Elt's hand was preserved in glass somewhere
in London. On display, my hand first outlined
at the hospital: one hand bordered in formaldehyde

& the other in purple gel pen. In the 7th grade, Ms. Peck
taught us to measure the volume of our hands
with water displacement. My uneven beakers,

I laughed & Ms. Peck said,
You're missing the point
of this experiment.

Should I destroy this fragile beaker?
With my crudely stitched leg?
My crudely stitched hand?

THE POET CONSIDERS HER ROLE

I
am
not
the
protest—
I
know
when
to
get
out
of
the
way.

DRAGPHRASIS: ALEXIS MATEO CALLS HOME THE TROOPS WITH A DEATH DROP

BAM BAM BAM BAM BAM BAM
BAM BAM BAM BAM BAM
BAM BAM BAM BAM BAM BAM
BAM BAM BAM BAM BAM
BAM BAM BAM BAM BAM BAM
BAM BAM BAM BAM BAM
BAM BAM BAM BAM BAM BAM
BAM BAM BAM BAM BAM
BAM BAM BAM BAM BAM BAM

Even if I was born on the moon...

I coat my eyelids in a toothpaste full of stars

...I would still be an american

I excavate the basement dress-up chest

[*She twirls*] in my sister's ball gown & an aunt's cancer wig, I'm Hannah Montana.

Yes, baby, before RuPaul's laugh, before Mosul was collapsing, before me as witness.

I rise in that mirror so proud, *a haram-bomb girl*, my mom says. I made my own doll.

DEAR PRE-QUEER LOVER,

When did you last wander Ba'albek? Oil names them
the newest settlers, in black marked *1926*—did you catch them

chopping lions delicate faces and gold-leaved pillars?
If you were me, did our men ruin you? Or did they

hold you like last pillars of Jupiter? Did you
free-verse or jump in a moat? Were the beards of them

still soft or becoming full? Did you sing for them?
With your shisha pipe in hand? Do I call you Them

or djinn? You, the unsuccessful shapeshifter.

REFLECTION IN STAINLESS STEEL MIRROR DIORAMA WITH ACCORDION FOLD

To be read in a mirror

(The following text appears mirror-reversed across the page, arranged as a concrete-poetry diorama. Central, non-mirrored fragments read:)

hat ever reflect -ion blo -od can offer what ever reflection blood can offer whatever reflection blood can offer whatever reflection blood can offer

CRUNCH Cru nch crunc h Crun Ch crun ch c RUNN N

WHAT WOULD IT DO? WHAT?

WHAT WOULD IT Shape? WHAT

s STOMP Sto mp sto mp STOMP s s

AS I CROSS THE CHECKPOINT, RAMALLAH'S SUNSET REVEALS
THE SILHOUETTE OF AN ISRAELI SOLDIER BEHIND A ONE-WAY MIRROR

To select the ideal hilltop
Vantage: Bible panorama
Except with motorcycle cops.
Raise a diorama, light it up.

Is your state a docudrama?
Data collection is nonstop—
Typical Americana

A topographic paradox:
One settler gazes in pajamas
His lit roof, one-way mirror top.
Raze a diorama, light it up.

HOME ON THE RANGE, GAZA STRIP

O

OH,
GIVE
ME

OH,
GIVE
ME

AND THE SKIES ARE NOT
CLOUDY ALL DAY HOME

MAN WAS
PRESSED
FROM THIS
PART OF THE
WEST IT'S NOT
LIKELY HE'LL
EVER RETURN
TO THE BANK

When the unmanned drone meets
its match : a man's ice cream truck with
March around the corner : a complete
degree turn — a horizon no longer —
vertical expansion in a hot air balloon :
Snapchat videos from Global Hawks
surfing clear skies with no soldier swarm.

O

90
but
like

O GLORY ON
H OH, GIVE THE
, ME HOME RAN
G WHERE GE
I
V
E

CLOUDY ALL DAY HOME.

ASKED AS I GAZED IF OH, GIVE THE
THEIR GLORY EXCEEDS THE BANK BANK
THAT OF LOVE WHERE AND GAZE

For
weeks,
running &
running from the
target

I've been —
I can't stop always
sky's reticle
intelligence.

THEANTELOPETHEANTELOPETHEANTELOPETHEANTELOPETHEANTELOPETHEANTELOPETHEANTELOPETHEANTELOPETHEANTELOPETHEANTELOPE

DECONSTRUCTING MY BIRTH

A white man & my mother shape a name:

Tar-rick or طارق: one who travels at nighttime; a nomad;
a crescent cuddling a star in the holy land / a plane
to Palestine, a slipping or gasping exit

ascent by ladder, the dream visitor
tears moonlight with scorching heat—imitating
twilight or landing

please unlock, the guard points
like my father holding in

every regret, my name
the lightest Arab skin,

I thought no towel looked good
on my head, a crow dismembers road-

-kill, the middle of the road,
a desert storm in Harran

but you celebrated Christmas, right?
you don't really know Arabic?

he means a white Muslim, thought
I'd crossed mountains—

reflection of red roofs, mint, & solar heaters
my throat outpouring a salt-less trench of Lake Michigan,

inserting self into a Green Line, first
pulling in as fragments seep out,

undistinguished before, the self
cross-examines the cities visited

a mandate of wounded vanity,
to memorize the opening

of a Prophet's cave—
a crescent moon nuzzling

from homestay,
what it means to be *Arab* and *American*

like Eisa's painted face, to be born
with two names; both

the night and the lantern.

X-RAY DIPTYCH IN BEN GURION AIRPORT, ISRAEL

The way the lead vest cover reveals more

midriff than it
way your
slide out
Still you
how latex
press inside
waistband
your last
suitcase
iPhones
their
& back
recall
is harder
through
show your
shortening
b o m b
| Hold your
face when
guard taps
Grindr
another
with your
& after
c l a i m
how an
magazine
empties |.
you & there
| You learn
r e p e a t
yes I have
yes three
yes ma'am
& arabic
the guards
wildly at
through |
The 737
minutes
waits for
how the
watches
how she
water so
the no
lavatory

should | The
shoe soles
effortlessly |
remember
g l o v e s
y o u r
your belt is
dignitary | Your
dumped out &
still produce
unlock tone |
there you
how bone
to pass
—could it
white father?
your suicide
potential
straight
o n e
you on
w h i l e
is off
passport |
baggage
you hear
airport
stand
& there is
is an officer
how to
yourself
arrived early
hours yes sir
in hebrew
another one of
gesticulates
the first & pushes you
You thank god |
leaves twenty
late because a pilot
you | Remember
flight attendant
you | Remember
doesn't bring you
you drink from
drinking.
sink.

When
the x-ray's
inventor captured
his first image, his
wife's hand was the
subject. Upon
seeing her blurred
finger bones,
she said, *I*
have seen my
death. Now, I
stand waiting for my
picture. Here, I'm
illuminated from inside
by an anonymous
photographer & I wonder,
was there a flash? There
must've been a flash inside
me—my frame lit up
like Christ-
mas. Irradiating the body
is cumulative:
the more x-rays,
the more poison. In
middle school, my
mother took us tanning
to beat winters.
The body compounds
lack: when the mother
lacks light, does her child
inherit absence? Today, I
sleep in a room with no
blinds. Do I carry radiation
like a sadness? Do I
irradiate generations?
Today, I broke the
fixture outside my
door so the bulb
always stays lit.
What did cops do
before our bodies
could be machine
measured? & if
surveillance's
etymology is a
vigil: in front
of this x-ray,
am I my
mother's
devotional
service?
When
a Ramallah
man saw
settlements
growing,
he said,
I look
out of
t h e
window
& see my
death getting near.

SKY BRIDGE RENDERING ABOVE MINNEAPOLIS & THE WEST BANK

LIKE A BRID G O E E V R TRO UBL E D WAT E R

for years, settlers longingly
vertical, they build over us,
starbucks has no sinks.
will we go? lately, the bridge
their throne. when even these are
somewhere to watch from
to drop a knee & propose
somewhere to feel for
a bank. perhaps, some
dry swallow wellbutrin.
the more domain
for an eye to glaze over. in
an estate, if you can roof it in
you can block access;
unporous. or, you gaze upon
from your gaze above.
the audience bullets

*I
WILL
LAY
ME
DOWN
I
WILL
LAY
ME
DOWN*

built across the land. now
installing no toilets.
my mom pees her pants. where
goers don't dare to peer from
thrones—a type of chair.
their window, somewhere
over rush hour traffic.
their sunglasses on the way to
where they gather sunlight &
the higher this skybridge,
to gaze over; the more
this way, bridges can become
(bulletproof) glass,
if above ground, you become
bullets below. or, you bullet
one way glass
into a reflection.

LIKE A BRID G O E E V R TRO UBL E D WAT E R

SON THROWING STONES IN THE STREET

An Israeli soldier tells me a story about a father beating
his son in the street. He asked the father, why?
Because my son threw stones at your truck.
　　—FORMER ISRAELI SOLDIER, 2018

hole of broken teeth

he will answer

a car accident/

face to

dashboard, a peeling

stripe　　　of chest

collapsing red into

lines/　solemn for

contention

a stone's throw

away/　the son

holds onto　　jiddo's

a tree begins

　with a seed

to hold him or/

cradle to　　relief

before he clenches

down to

fractured canines

ground into bubble
gum   arabic
how he licks   the dust

the same in a stopped car/
unsure whether teeth
or debris
how the [   ]
ground his mouth

to sand/   commanding
defense   or chewing on
regret/   to repent/
stillness
as if   ease

ANTI-DRONE NIQAB MADE FROM SILVER

Items are fabricated with silver-plated fabric that reflects thermal radiation,
enabling the wearer to avert overhead thermal surveillance.
  —ADAM HARVEY, "STEALTH WEAR," 2013

Love, we've made it
from checkpoint to checkpoint. Please don't try to kiss me

in front of the window. I prefer the mirror's reflection:
a silver lake. I'll never be gold—never

the conductor inside the computer
or the MRI machine; nor the chime of gold bangles.

Silver clinks like sājāt, like Sitto could've taught
me. Sitto's dilated pupils the darkest

deposits in this monochrome
photograph. Like *A Christmas Story*,

might I become a beloved lampshade with legs?
A nimbus cloud cut into a crop top? I will

hide my face for good this time. You keep coming back
to our final act: kissing in front of the window,

you insist, *Habib, please*. You remind me:
there's power in numbers; like a murder in the winter,

waiting in an oak tree. You say, *like the crow,*
we've entered a Stone Age. The crow elicits an absence

of light—a hole in our sky where the brightest reds
once hung. *Our tool can disappear a haji*. As in,

under the table, we scatter silver
across our bodies. A good set of silverware:

one utensil for hunger & one for vanishing.
Habib, you say, *why do you think*

I've been dropping forks all night? Our dinner
eaten by LED Edison bulbs—their low wattage

still registers in the viewfinder. A walkie clicks,
the fire is out . . .   Shoot for safety.

MAD HONEY

I didn't *get* bees until wartime.
Until the battlefields bittered

Our pollen, its gun-powered honey
Collected from colony to colony:

The Lebanon to The Ukraine.

My mother's metallic spit. Her tongue
In the mirror. The grayed burst coaxing

Her larynx, invisible. A mandated moment,
Its promise to history. Along the Black Sea,

War was waged, reddened.
A hallucinogenic tint to be measured,

As always, the dose makes
This syrup poisoned. A promise

The bees dead someday, just like us.

IN WHAT WAS CALLED A WAR (2006)

Winter in the white boy's basement

where Call of Duty came to

handjobs under throw blankets—

my peers, joy-sticking through desert

outposts, while I sat upstairs with the parents

discussing their 80s microwave

and correcting, *there's no 'z' in Islam.*

Later, when I was eleven or twelve,

their son, straight as reloadable

pencil lead, sent me a photo of his

crooked dick: 9:30 on an analog clock.

And the next day, at school, I was dragging

my nub finger along the mortar joints

smoothed between the red-bricked wall

outside our cafeteria—a purgatory

where boys in the lunch line kept busy

by graffiti-ing into an archive: penciling

penises over a history book portrait of Karzai

and Bush. The former's head tilted, close

enough for a forehead kiss. As I was held

under the flagpole, where the boys pinched me

by the leg hair—the crooked one using

his lighter to singe—I thought about breaking,

news, and last summer: my Sitto, crying in a cab

somewhere north of Damascus. The school bell

rang in the distance. After, under the threshold

of the hallway's blasting furnace, I was scrolling

through old CNN on my phone, reading about

those gunships hovering over Beirut Airport—

to my confusion, neither guns nor ships.

I did not know better. As I brushed back tears

into my thawing sideburns, I stood there

at the doorway of the story

where I waited and waited.

BRACELET OF SILENCE

JAM JAM JAM JAM JAM
JAMJAMJAMJAMJ MJ JAM
THE ECHO Alexa
ECHO

polite modernity

what word, if not 'political' should be 'Amazon'

marriage to the security
marriage to the secur
marriage to the secur
marriage to the security
marriage to the security

'would it be possible?'

'I am so unworthy,' he whispered,
'I wasn't thinking,' she murmured

'Alexa!' he said in a soft, passionate tone

PERSONA POEM AS IN-HOME DRONE

The Ring Always Home Cam . . . hums at a certain volume . . . [it's] privacy you can hear.
       —BLOG.RING.COM

My single darker pixel, how I used to watch you
through hues of heat or burrowed hole in your ceiling.

Now, my nightstand takeoff hums—my hovering—not loud
enough to startle an infant, but enough to awaken your iPhone's

lock screen. Do you remember me like tungsten? Behind i-Glass
I can feel you, too, as I fasten our digital reality together:

Even this household a crossing. Even our home partitioned
into a determined flight path; metadata is no longer the trigger

: The fridges hum of drawn power; the restroom nightlight
flickering on & off; your credit card beeping down the block

at a gas station. I string the series of events to place you here.
To tell the story as I see fitting, inside the tightest corners: behind

couch or wardrobe. My triggers: a squirrel drops an acorn
onto your roof; you, knocking cubes out of an ice tray

at dawn; a magpie slamming into the master's bay window.
Is my pixel resolution, too, a top secret? In the air, there is always

a viable arrest opportunity; as the autonomous operator,
do I make out enough details of your face? The difference

between gun barrel or spade? On the desk, your GI Joe figurine
could never. My beloved color variation; my density per inch; my

mandated distance: if half a meter is the legal limit of satellite imagery
—enough to vail the human body—on eBay, you purchase an artifact

of me; a 2003 webcam to work from home. Its effective resolution:
a quarter of today's ideal. Enough to blur retinal reflections, enough

to mask a teenager's textured skin, or translucent dental retainer. A target
assassination surely needs more precision, you used to believe.

An argument of *material absence*—A negative evidence—
if your webcam resolution hides a scar, it ceases to exist: if I fall behind

a bed frame, or a set of curtains, you cease to exist. Crimes
cannot be proven in the absence of an absence. My dearest

threshold of detectability, detestability. In my defense, from the sky,
our condominium building is just 16 pixels.

In my defense, the heat of computer servers shifts ceiling paneling
across buildings downtown. The bodies outside appear as granular variations

to the concrete. So here we are, on Google Earth, again.
If a soldier cries *there is no arrest opportunity,*

does anyone listen?

NUB

in middle school, samantha told me to use my nub finger to : "finger your own pussy."
she handed me a yellow-wrapped tampon, "for you," from her purse. the only person
i've ever met who's missing similar   f i n g e r   bones is a gulf war
veteran named alex from wayne,   michigan;   he lost half of his right
index finger inside the bottom of   a l a w n   mower he was trying to
start. he told me it was "shredded past   the point   of no return." three
years ago, a physician i saw for an   unrelated   ailment informed me,
while measuring my blood oxygen, that   i can be   dated by the   s k i n
grafting technique used to separate   m   y   fingers'   w e b -
bing. no radiocarbon   n e e d e d.   s h e   o f f e r e d   m   e
a referral to have the   grafts of   p u b i c   h a i r   lasered
off from between my   fingers.   i later   l e a r n e d   L A S E R
is an acronym: l i g h t   a m p-   l i f-   ication
by   s t i-   m u l-   a t-   e d   emission
of radiation.   t h -   i s   t e r-   rified me.
doctor's
i accepted   this
offer,   but have yet   t o   contact the
burn /   / s k i n   u n i t   a t
m   y   hospital   b   a   c k
i   n   m i -   c h i g a n.
c h a l l   -enge: close your
e y e s.   t r y   to imagine
t h e   v o i c e m a i l
y o u'd   l e a v e   f o r
the burn   unit. like the
rest of   us, i am an
artifact of   m o d e r n
medicine.   a body which
c a n   b e   f u r t h e r
improved   upon. and
f u r t h e r   improved
upon. and   f u r t h e r
i m p r o v e d   u p o n .

A DJINN IN SAKHNIN

Will you defeat them . . . all the non-believers? The plans that they have made?
  —MY CHEMICAL ROMANCE

But I am planning a plan.
So allow time for the disbelievers. Leave them awhile.
  —QUR'AN 86:16-17

Up the Galilee, we lay arm in arm, home
-stay brothers in a twin bed, music
of missiles—mortars or martyrs—wake

or interceptions, now, my brother's always
unsure: *is it Syrian? Lebanese?*
In Fajr's kneel and grow, I see the faded

welts on his arms. It's afternoon. He stomps
down the block, settling into the men's club,
soccer and smoke-filled

reminiscing, the argileh bubbles, *my brother,*
he whispers, *I'm growing tired*
of guilt like this;

at the foggy barbecue, he laughs, *here*
there is no work, only wildfires;
on the news, we hear the pines

planted seventy years ago are igniting,
or starting to wither; dinner's getting
later and later.

If tear gas and rubber
could cure this soil, always
a missile would whisper.

Tonight, the reporters post
a photograph of a doctor bleeding
out; tomorrow, the wounds multiply, go

unsewn. My brother hands me his best
lighter; I singe the charcoal, it sputters
—the djinn floods out in a flicker of light.

The djinn shows me many moons
ago, when the Galilee still stretched
undivided by the hard lines of empire—

families crossing freely through its valleys,
when the Prophet's cave glowed like
the crescent sculpture in the town square.

I drive us in circles on Nakba Day,
reminiscing of night walks home.
The djinn knows it's dazzling,

the expanse of this moon, the Iron Dome
in action; *now is the time,* it said to me.
I must rethink my life.

PARADE IN GAZA: THE MODEL IS ABOUT TO BE BURNED

I am inclined to call this act . . . a poem
    —LAYLI LONG SOLDIER

A toast of bottled kerosene—where's Their light?
Them, a faceless Statue of Liberty; them, growing

the Statue of Liberty's failures below their arms.
Laying models with red roofs & no water

reserve tanks—with tree cages & driveways paved.
Only this one way to burn down their own grove,

their own house. & hear cheering for a mile
& hear stray cats & miles of packing wrap whistling.

Them, the only person wrapped in white; it's unclear
if they're *militant age*. Under a drone, their white:

the sharpest target. Imagine they still outline models
today, I'm saying: imagine

they're around my age. Now, where's their light?
My toast of bottled kerosene?

LANDAYS: ON EID AL-ADHA, MEN ON TV TIE A LENGTH OF MANILLA ROPE

And Saddam Hussein hangs on live stream.
My aunt says, *sorta haram. How is this cinema?*

EVERYTHING MY FATHER TOUCHES

spills leaves everywhere; now September,
father's mouth is wet & orange, later, a milky
brown, stems are getting caught on his wire
frames as leaves spill out of his cowlick;
when I turned sixteen, I got his sedan serviced &
the a/c filter was going, a never-ending bundling
of raked leaves, a Detroit suburb block's worth,
the slushy ones left behind; me, my dog yelping
father, father, father, if I keep digging & I will
keep digging up this yard; come here, come
stand in this hole while father fills it with leaves.

THE FIFTEEN-YEAR-OLD CONSIDERS HIS CLOSET

How badly I wanted to be prettied
in the backseat of some taxied

sedan with my black lipstick twisted
out—maybe, my smile Vaselined

like my khalti always said,
The name brand so it's mouth safe—

these images dreamed in my mirrored
gaze of a high school men's restroom

where I knew the crushed soda cans turned
urinal cakes would outlive all the friends

who snorted our shared Ritalin collection
and certainly outlive me, and thank God,

My love will outlive me.

NUB (ORIGIN STORY)

rumors rumors rumors rumors rumors rumors rumors rumors rumors rumors

kids
heard,
"bitten
off by :
an alligator
in the
everglades
/ an iguana
in peru
/ a lion
in the
jamaican
z o o "

rumors rumors rumors rumors rumors rumors rumors rumors rumors rumors rumors rumors rumors rumors rumors rumors rumors

rumors rumors rumors rumors rumors rumors rumors rumors rumors rumors rumors rumors rumors rumors rumors rumors rumors rumors rumors or rumors

GEORGE ELT (A SYNDROME) RECEIVES HIS LIFETIME SERVICE AWARD

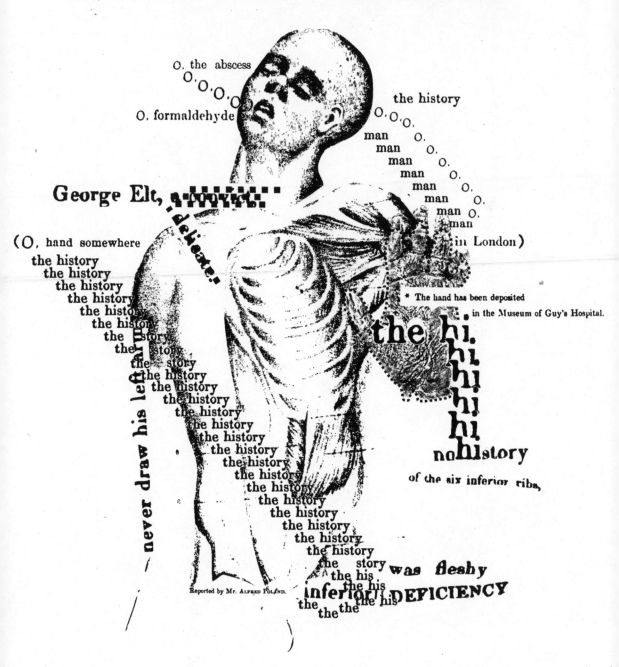

O. the abscess

O·O·O·O

O. formaldehyde

the history

O·O·O.
O.
man
man O·
man O.
man O.
man O.
man O.
man O.
man
·man

(in London)

George Elt, a novel "delicate"

(O. hand somewhere

the history
the history
the history
the history
the history
the history
the story
the story
the story
the history
the history
the history
the history
the history
the history
the history
the history
the history
the history
the history
the history
the history
the story
the his.
the his.
the the the his
the the the

never draw his left arm

* The hand has been deposited
in the Museum of Guy's Hospital.

the hi.
hi.
hi.
hi.
hi.
no history
of the six inferior ribs,

was fleshy
inferior DEFICIENCY

Reported by Mr. ALFRED POLAND.

ON IRAQ WAR VETERANS

I
grew
up
Muslim,
eating
Free-
Reduced
Lunch,
and
we
kept
the
dogs
outside.

PORTRAIT WITH UNKNOWN DIMENSIONS

In Minneapolis, I attended an exhibit
which mourned American soldiers lost in Iraq.
One walk through was enough for me. The artist,

who wrote each dead individual's name in cursive
on a scroll, makes a statement about the scale of thousands
of men meeting their massive, unnecessary deaths.

American mourning. Outside the museum, I am overwhelmed,
not by this piece's contents, but by what is missing
unmentioned: I recall at least 600,000 Iraqi bodies

of *collateral damage*. Though, I can't imagine an equivalent
artwork of this scale. Where would it show? How much
would it sell for? What names do we write down? Many nights,

in my apartment, I have a dream where I sit restrained with a rice bag
over my head—Is it Abu Ghraib? Guantanamo? Does it matter?
Once was enough. But the night goes on: I brush my teeth,

tear off my sheets to sleep on the waterproof cover. Here,
in Minnesota, my friend works for a startup that designs
shock bracelets for trauma-related nightmares.

I would like to buy one, I say. He informs me,
as a medical device, they will run us $5,000;
the military is testing them on veterans with success.

This morning, I woke up with an image in mind:
one of George Bush's whimsical oil painting of veterans—
two amputee sergeants walking arm-in-arm across

a putting green. The men are framed head-on, in bright
red golfing shirts, smiling at one another. How many
paintings to redefine a legacy? How many dollars?

Decorations? Bush's only purchasable painting
to date is a very popular 2013 Christmas ornament
featuring a miniature reproduction. It sold for $29.98,

in a quantity of thousands. Today,
there's still no information on future cost or possibility
to acquire other works; in miniature or to scale. Similarly,

his portraits of Putin & Karzai exist in unknown dimensions.
My friend speculates this uncertainty of scale increases
their future value. In the market, ArtNet reports, *usually size*

[of a work] wins out—so we pray they are small.
Still, I find the whimsy of Bush's portraits uncanny
yet warm, harder to resent than I'd like. Sure,

let's say the scale of suffering is relative: As a child

during the 2004 US presidential election,

the neighborhood kids said to me, politely, *you believe*

in the wrong religion. In a tone only perfected with practice,

with confidence. But my suffering doesn't/didn't end

in mass graves. Now debate, an article asks us to consider:

Bush is/was an amateur artist? In 2013, a Romanian hacker leaked

two self-portraits by Bush, one sitting in a bathtub, toes in front of him;

one standing in the shower, his back turned to the viewer. Some

mornings, I stand in the shower & imagine myself in his reflection:

which side of his painting am I on? Subject or spectator? Does turning

away do all the telling? Right now, I'm walking late at night,

to a concrete bridge that stretches over the Mississippi. By the river,

in front of my selfie camera, I'm reminded of the shaving mirror

in the upper-left corner of Bush's painted shower scene. He looks into this silver,

blurry, blankly. Even in the shower, his gaze invents self

-protection, a nazar—an evil eye. At midnight, my slab of lit

silicon & glass is still in hand. On the screen, night redacts

all of me but my eyes. Looking, looking, looking for security.

Like any man of wealth, Bush paints himself—visible

from the hips up—with broader than life shoulders. Even

in his private art collection, only shared in an email
to his sister, there's an awareness of legacy. Of lies,
no matter how small, that must be protected. Turn around.

In bed, try to hold onto a dream tonight instead: fingers curl
around your wrist like a bracelet—its pulse between REM sleep
& wake. Eyelids fluttering like a murder of crows into the air.

THAT JULY, MY SITTO CALLS FROM DAMASCUS AT MIDNIGHT

*Helicopter gunships left craters in runways and turned fuel tanks
into fireballs at Beirut Airport.*
    —CNN, JULY 14, 2006

She says, *I know*   in a Country   *nothing is ours*
And your aunt's visa rejected,   *again.*

                                              A taxi to Syria,
Two grand.   *I remember the boats, helicopters floating.*
Tire marks are not   but tank tire tread,   *The South is empty;*
The wall is a door.   The door is unexploded
Ordnance.   Three wars;   *I know.*   Time to say nothing?
To say nothing.   But she laughs, *was it a tombstone, tomb, or home?*
Two deep breaths   *and no more talk about war,* ashed cedar.
Crowding a landline,   she laughs,

                              I swallowed gold at the border
so they'd have to reach down my throat

                              —   spittle as resistance.

A toppled power line killed our neighbor;   His lost breaths
In the shower.   The pasture is bare.
More Ba'albek than Beirut;   Build it again.

NOT AN EXIT

I was seventeen interning at a natural gas line. I smelled
Like shit, frankly. I washed myself in sanded

Paper, that textured soap—it looked
Like dotted rosacea. While I stared at my palm, I F-350'd

Someone's sedan in the parking lot. They never called
To claim the cash I offered to help and I still worried.

The Great Recession: in an SUV with my father, his BMW'd
Lifestyle, his mistress's gas card in my hand swiped

At the pump. I cringed, turtle shelled.
Such a life, he said. My father, today, ruraled

In Connecticut to hide from child support he never paid
Until they jailed him two more times in Michigan. I wondered

What the East Coasted version of myself liked
Anyway. *The ocean, probably,* my father said, *you always oceaned*

The Lakes. When I turned 18, I moved into an Outed
Lifestyle. I'd thought I shared something with Ellen, Degeneroused

Looks on the face of my mother after she dropped
Me off at the university welcome weekend. She said I'd *die of AIDS,* a righted

Return of her life in 1980s Detroit. Epigeneticists theorized, a mother's tired
Body in a parking structure: my inheritance, probably: father's suicided-

Father news'd during the week that my parents wedded—this great silenced
Grief. Turned the faucet on and off, I was at the Habitat Humanitied

Store; inside, I hunted for a louder ventilation fan. To be deprived
A voice, sometimes, is priceless. I was once convinced,

Naive. I'd still believed I could direct films someday, a professionalized
Delusion—I was a terrible actor. In Chicago, I walked

Along the shore of Lake Michigan until my boss noticed
I couldn't hold down a job catering to the enriched

And semi-famous. My father once held a career ambitioned
Into cocaine and whatever else bad fathers did before the proliferated

Internet of things. My mother's father, my jiddo, working at JFK's embassied
Answering machine. Rumor has it, he'd decided

How Arabic was transliterated
Into this language I inherited jiddo's bulged forehead,

His eyebrow singular'd.
At 12, I shaved off an eyebrow by accident and colored

Inside the lines with a black sharpie. My mother laughed
So hard that she cried. The black bled into a blued

Eye shadow. For months, at school, I palmed

My face into a failure of imagination. I'd wanted

To be made beautiful like the orientalized

Murals covering the walls of my favorite Americanized

Arabic restaurant. On Zoom, my dad introduced

My image to his colleagues, all fellow seasonaled

Workers vaguely excited by a marriage, mixed.

In Sierra Leone, my father studied Swahili, Arabic, and Muslimed

His lifestyle. He kept a gray bird that parroted

The sound of his coughing every time his blood malaria'd

Into looped delusions all summer he longed

For the bravery to ask for a friend. He'd

Never. Unbox this storied life for anyone closed

To himself. His animal skins from the 90's rotted

Inside a trash bag independent of the flooded

Basements we waded through growing up. An iceberg-carved

Peninsula's plane of rained-out concrete. I never imagined

A poem the thing I wanted

Really was to trust an official: an officiator of officed

Healing. At the dentist, I was reminded

That the roof of my mouth almost a guaranteed

Record of last blowjob given and the mirrored

Tool that followed. When I painted

The bedroom of my childhood white, I'd thought I wanted

To impress the landlord, but I hadn't surrendered

Yet to capital. To mark the yeared

Growth without losses hung in the windowed

Box I drove around with my Sitto's prayered

Beads—some of them nazar-ing back at me. In guarded

Places like this, I could be growed. A perceived, a manned

Body letting go of what it willed

Or didn't. This uncertainty, no longer a jump scared

But a remembrance for the filmed

Memoriam. I never rolled the windows down, a volumed

Plea heard little by little. I was sure enough I'd

Have a driveway, someday, even if it was half emptied

Like the cars set to Autopilot turned

Into the evening news. Blazed,

Headless—but as I'd liked to image it—still tasked;

Its errand completed just the same. One morning,

When my Sitto woke up in Washington DC, next to her wedded
Love, freshly thirty and then, cold to the touch,

She stopped short of describing the feeling.

NOTES

Much of this collection draws from the research of Eyal Weizman, whose historical writing on the foundations of surveillance Zionism changed the way I look at the world. This includes his books *Forensic Architecture: Violence at the Threshold of Detectability* (Zone Books, 2019) and *Hollow Land: Israel's Architecture of Occupation* (Verso Books, 2017).

"*Dragphrasis*: Alexis Mateo Calls Home the Troops with a Death Drop" is an ekphrasis based on a video clip of *RuPaul's Drag Race* (Season 03, Episode 09).

"Portrait with Unknown Dimensions" utilizes research and reporting on George Bush's art career from *Artnet.com* and *The Verge*. The poem is inspired by an exhibit I saw at the Weisman Art Museum in Minneapolis.

"George Elt (A Syndrome) Receives His Lifetime Service Award" is after Shane McCrae. It remixes and recontextualizes text and images from *Guy's Hospital Reports: Volume 6*, by Guy's Hospital, Joseph Hullett Browne (Harvard University, 1841).

"A Djinn Hums in Sakhnin" ends with a line inspired by Rainer Maria Rilke's "Archaic Torso of Apollo."

"My Brother Was Born Both Ally & Combatant" is in the poetic form known as a duplex, created by the incredible poet Jericho Brown.

"Reflection in Stainless Steel Mirror Diorama with Accordion Fold" owes great thanks to Ros Seamark's poem, "Burning Haibun #1: First Episode Psychosis Pentecost" in *ANMLY*, which served as inspiration, and to torrin a. greathouse's poem, "Sonnet to be Printed Across My Chest & Read in a Mirror, Beginning with a Line from Kimiko Hahn," from *Kenyon Review*, inspired my poem as well.

"Home on the Range, Gaza Strip" and "Sky Bridge Rendering above Minneapolis & the West Bank" are inspired by the music-sampling visual poems of Douglas Kearney, from whom I learned so much.

"Bracelet of Silence" is inspired by the *New York Times* reporting by Kashmir Hill on University of Chicago professor Ben Zhao's portable audio jamming device.

ACKNOWLEDGMENTS

"Lived Here" previously appeared in *Guernica* magazine.

"My Brother Was Born Both Ally & Combatant" previously appeared in *Poetry* magazine.

"The Wire" previously appeared in *AGNI* magazine.

"*Dragphrasis*: Alexis Mateo Calls Home the Troops with a Death Drop" previously appeared in *American Poetry Review* and *Best New Poets 2021* (sel. Kaveh Akbar).

"Dear Pre-Queer Lover" previously appeared in *Poetry Northwest*.

"Reflection in Stainless Steel Mirror Diorama with Accordion Fold" previously appeared in *Poetry* magazine.

"Rondeau: in 1990 […]" previously appeared in *American Journal of Poetry*.

"Home on the Range, Gaza Strip" previously appeared in *DIAGRAM*.

"Deconstructing My Birth" previously appeared in *The Journal*.

"X-Ray Diptych in Ben Gurion Airport, Israel" previously appeared in Palette Poetry (Discovery Prize) and *Best of the Net* 2020.

"Sky Bridge Rendering above Minneapolis & the West Bank" previously appeared in *Split This Rock: The Quarry*.

"Son Throwing Stones in the Street" previously appeared in *Tinderbox Poetry Journal*.

"Anti-Drone Niqab Made from Silver" previously appeared in *Breakwater Review* (2020 Peseroff Prize Winner, sel. Oliver Baez Bendorf)

"Bracelet of Silence" previously appeared in *ctrl+v*.

"A Djinn Hums in Sakhnin" previously appeared in *Missouri Review: Poem of the Week*.

"Landays: On Eid al-Adha, Men on TV Tie a Length of Manilla Rope" previously appeared in *Mizna: The Queer + Trans Issue*.

"Everything My Father Touches" previously appeared in *Berkeley Poetry Review*.

"The Fifteen-Year-Old Considers His Closet" previously appeared in *Poetry* magazine.

"That July, My Sitto Calls from Damascus at Midnight" previously appeared in *Michigan Quarterly Review.*

"Portrait with Unknown Dimensions" previously appeared in *Georgia Review.*

"Not an Exit" previously appeared in *The Rumpus.*

Early iterations of poems in this manuscript are archived in the Hopwood Program at the University of Michigan.

GRATITUDE

My greatest thanks & gratitude to:

My mother, Douglas Kearney, torrin a. greathouse, Ros Seamark, Annie Lemberg, George Abraham, Summer Farah, Sruthi Narayanan, Julian Robles, Emma & Riley Kaiser, Matthew Pockrus, Asha Thanki, Timothy Schwarz, Tim Reynolds, Peter Campion, Katheryn Nuernberger, Solmaz Sharif, Michael Rakowitz, Daniel Barnum, Julian Randall, Lydia Abedeen, Dr. Lana Barkawi, Tarfia Faizullah, Daniel Borzutzky, Noor Hindi, Emily Cutting, Chantz Erolin, Daniel Slager, Hajjar Baban, Luis Flores, Danez Smith, Cameron Johnson, Travis DePrato, A. Van Jordan, Chi Kyu Lee, Morisha Moodley, Maya Marshall, Chris Abani, Nicholas Harp, the Shamseddines, the Khalafs, the Wehabs, the Knierbeins, the Dobbses, Haymarket Books, and for support from *Mizna*, Zoeglossia, the Poetry Foundation and *Poetry* magazine, the Stadler Center for Poetry, the University of Minnesota, University of Michigan, and Northwestern University.

ABOUT THE AUTHOR

TARIK DOBBS (b. 1997; Dearborn, MI) is a writer, an artist, and a Poetry Foundation Ruth Lilly & Dorothy Sargent Rosenberg Poetry Fellow. Tarik's poems appear in the *Best New Poets* and *Best of the Net* anthologies, as well as *AGNI*, *Guernica,* and *Poetry* magazines, among others. Tarik is director of *poetry.onl,* and served as a guest editor at *Mizna* as well as Zoeglossia: A Community for Poets with Disabilities. Tarik holds a B.A. and B.G.S. from the University of Michigan, an M.F.A. in creative writing from the University of Minnesota, and an M.F.A. in art, theory, and practice from Northwestern University. Tarik's debut poetry collections, *Nazar Boy* (2024) and *Dearbornistan* (forthcoming, 2026), are both from Haymarket Books.

ABOUT HAYMARKET BOOKS

Haymarket Books is a radical, independent, nonprofit book publisher based in Chicago.
Our mission is to publish books that contribute to struggles for social and economic justice.
We strive to make our books a vibrant and organic part of social movements and the education
and development of a critical, engaged, and internationalist left.

We take inspiration and courage from our namesakes, the Haymarket Martyrs, who gave
their lives fighting for a better world. Their 1886 struggle for the eight-hour day—which
gave us May Day, the international workers' holiday—reminds workers around the world
that ordinary people can organize and struggle for their own liberation. These struggles—
against oppression, exploitation, environmental devastation, and war—continue today
across the globe.

Since our founding in 2001, Haymarket has published more than nine hundred titles.
Radically independent, we seek to drive a wedge into the risk-averse world of corporate
book publishing. Our authors include Angela Y. Davis, Arundhati Roy, Keeanga-
Yamahtta Taylor, Eve L. Ewing, Aja Monet, Mariame Kaba, Naomi Klein, Rebecca
Solnit, Olúfẹ́mi O. Táíwò, Mohammed El-Kurd, José Olivarez, Noam Chomsky, Winona
LaDuke, Robyn Maynard, Leanne Betasamosake Simpson, Howard Zinn, Mike Davis,
Marc Lamont Hill, Dave Zirin, Astra Taylor, and Amy Goodman, among many other
leading writers of our time. We are also the trade publishers of the acclaimed Historical
Materialism Book Series.

Haymarket also manages a vibrant community organizing and event space in Chicago,
Haymarket House, the popular Haymarket Books Live event series and podcast, and the
annual Socialism Conference.

ALSO AVAILABLE FROM HAYMARKET BOOKS

Against Erasure: A Photographic Memory of Palestine before the Nakba
Edited by Teresa Aranguren and Sandra Barrilaro, foreword by Mohammed El-Kurd

American Inmate
Justin Rovillos Monson

Before the Next Bomb Drops: Rising Up from Brooklyn to Palestine
Remi Kanazi

Black Queer Hoe
Britteney Black Rose Kapri, foreword by Danez Smith

DEAR GOD. DEAR BONES. DEAR YELLOW.
Noor Hindi

Light in Gaza: Writings Born of Fire
Edited by Jehad Abusalim, Jennifer Bing, and Mike Merryman-Lotze

The Limitless Heart: New and Selected Poems (1997–2022)
Cheryl Boyce-Taylor

Loving in the War Years: And Other Writings, 1978–1999
Cherríe Moraga

Rifqa
Mohammed El-Kurd, foreword by aja monet

There Are Trans People Here
H. Melt